Jen's

Green Frugal Living

53 SIMPLE LIFEHACKS TO SAVE $2,500+ A MONTH

Jennifer Malone

Copyright © 2024 – *Valley of Joy Publishing Press*

All Rights Reserved.

No part of this publication may be reproduced, stored in a retrieval system or transmitted in any form or by any means, electronic, mechanical, photocopying, recording or otherwise, without the proper written consent of the copyright holder, except brief quotations used in a review.

Published by:

Valley Of Joy Publishing Press

COVER & INTERIOR DESIGN

BY

ANGELLA SITOMPUL

FIRST EDITION

Disclaimer

This book may contain content or images created with the assistance of artificial intelligence (AI) technology. All AI-assisted content complies with Amazon KDP's guidelines, and we have made every effort to ensure that any AI-created materials meet high standards of quality and originality. Each piece has been reviewed, edited, and curated to provide value and enhance the book's subject matter.

Legal Notice

Valley of Joy Publishing House retains full ownership and copyright of all AI-assisted content in this book. Any resemblance to copyrighted materials, trademarks, or actual persons—living or deceased—is purely coincidental. All content has been created with the intention of originality and complies with applicable copyright and intellectual property laws. Unauthorized reproduction, distribution, or use of this material is strictly prohibited.

Thank you for understanding and supporting the integration of AI in creative works.

CONTENTS

Introduction 8

    Why I Wrote This Book 10

    What's Inside This Book 11

    How to Ensure Life-long Habits 16

Chapter 1: Home: 6 Ways to Save as Much as $157.03 a Month 18

    Cloth Napkins 19

    Paper Towels 21

    Cleaning Supplies 23

    Reusable Water Bottles 26

    Lawn Care 27

    Install a Rain Barrel 28

    Even More Ways to Save 29

        Try Xeriscaping 30

        Install a Bidet 33

        Use a Toaster Oven 34

Chapter 2: Food And Grocery: 6 Ways to Save as Much as $316 per Month 35

Reusable Coffee Pods 36

Meal Planning 37

Food Waste Strategy 38

Bring Your Own Bag 39

Buy in Bulk 40

Bulk Buying Tips 42

Shop Online 43

Vacuum Seal Foods 46

Tips to Save Even More 47

Chapter 3: Body and Beauty: 6 Ways to Save as Much as $39.04 per Month 51

Shampoo Bars 52

Refillable Containers 54

Washable Cotton Rounds 55

Subscription Boxes 56

Make Your Own 57

Using a Reusable Tissue Pack 59

More Ways to Save Money 61

Chapter 4: Energy: 8 Ways to Save as Much to $108.31 per Month 65

LED Lighting 66

Turn Down the Water Heater.................................68

Program Your Thermostat 69

Energy-efficient Curtains.......................................69

Smart Power Strips 72

Take Shorter Showers 74

Use that Dishwasher 75

Dry Your Clothes Outside 76

More Ways to Save Even More 77

Chapter 5: Transportation: 5 Ways to Save as Much as $1,017.82 per Month 81

Take the Bus or Subway 82

Hop on That Bike 85

Turn the Car Engine Off...85

Wash Your Car by Hand 86

Even More Ways to Save 88

Chapter 6: Clothing: 5 Ways to Save as Much as $274.91 per Month 92

Online Consignment 93

Save with Cost-per-wear.......................................95

    Shop Thrift Stores 96

    Rent that Dress 97

    Snatch Up Brand Names for Less...98

    Even More Ways to Save 99

Chapter 7: Entertainment: 7 Ways to Save as Much as $272.77 per Month *103*

    The Library..103

    Free Movies 107

    Free Classes or Workshops..109

    Cable Costs 110

    Even More Ways to Save...112

Chapter 8: Renovations and Interior Decorating: 6 Ways to Save as Much as $235.65 per Month..*115*

    Insulation 116

    Buy Used Furniture 119

    Make Your Own Furniture...120

    Repaint Your Furniture 121

    Repurpose Ordinary Containers 122

    Bamboo Flooring 122

    Ways to Save More 124

Chapter 9: Miscellaneous Tips: 4 Ways to Save as Much as $97.33 per Month *127*

    Grow Your Own Vegetables **128**

    Cloth Diapers **129**

    Invest in an Energy-Efficient Water Heater.........................**131**

    Recycle Your Cellphone..**132**

    Ways to Save More..**133**

Conclusion *136*

INTRODUCTION

We all want to be good stewards of the planet. If given the chance, we'd choose an environmentally friendly activity or project over one that hurts Mother Nature. At least, I would like to think we would. The planet needs our help—now more than ever.

The statistics are stark—and frightening. We've just experienced the hottest year ever recorded: 2023. Deforestation—the cutting down of trees is happening at an alarming rate. Those are just two threats to our environment.

Though we want to help the planet, we worry that the

costs would burden your family and personal finances. And we sigh, believing our paltry efforts wouldn't make a difference.

And who can afford to spend money to aid in saving the environment? The price of nearly everything has risen. Grocery shopping means paying more on every visit. Clothing costs have risen. And we all know utilities take a larger and larger chunk out of your budget every month.

What if I told you that the total opposite is true? That way, you can save the planet and money simultaneously. And that even the smallest of efforts can have a significant effect on the environment.

It's true. And it doesn't involve making a significant shift in your lifestyle. A little change here; a little change there. The next thing you know, you're acting even more environmentally friendly and saving money. It's a win-win.

Don't worry that your seemingly small acts won't matter. Even the smallest of acts contribute to a healthier world.

I speak from experience. For nearly a decade, I've been

using tricks and tips to save money. Only about a year into my changes, I realized that my new-found habits were also good for the environment.

Why I Wrote This Book

By the time I figured this out, I was already the author of many online articles about saving money painlessly. I had been a guest speaker for local groups. And people started calling me "The Money Saver." Individuals would stop me at the supermarket, asking my opinion on the best deal. They would email me asking for help getting them out of debt.

I couldn't believe it took me as long as it did to realize that every time I added another money-saving habit, I also contributed a small amount to saving the planet. And you know what? It felt good. Every person who adopted one of my strategies also made an impact, however small, on the environment.

It inspired and challenged me. How could I help even more people save money and create a larger, positive impact on the planet?

This book is the result of inspiration and challenge.

You're already interested in this idea if you're reading this book. And maybe you're already making slight changes in your habits. This book will help you focus on the areas where you can make a genuine difference while furthering your money.

WHAT'S INSIDE THIS BOOK

Here's what you can expect to find.

In Chapter 1, I discuss the 6 ways you can save as much as $157.91 a month with small changes around your home. Here's a look at what you can expect:

• The one surprising way you can reduce your water bill—and it doesn't involve limiting your shower time.

• Paper towels and paper napkins hurt the environment—and cost you money. You'll be astonished at how much they cost over a year. But wait…I have an alternative.

• Discover the one little kitchen appliance that can save you up to 12 percent on your energy bill. You probably already have one in your home.

Have you seen the price of groceries lately? Yes, I have. That's why Chapter 2 provides you with 6 strategies to help you save as much as $316 monthly. Here are just a few of the tips you'll find in this chapter:

• K-cups make a good cup of coffee, but they burden your wallet and the environment. This one little trick will solve both those problems.

• Discover one change in your shopping habits that can save you as much as $125 a month.

• Fresh herb prices got you down? Make this one change and enjoy the savings.

If you're spending more money than you care about bath and beauty products, you'll want to read Chapter 3. I present 6 ways you can save up to $39.04 a month. Here, you'll discover:

• How you can save on shampoo costs with this one type of shampoo that doesn't come in a plastic bottle

• Discover how to eliminate your need for disposable

tissues. It's a saner, sanitary way to cut your costs and help.

• There's a dirty little secret about test sample bottles. They're not recyclable. But this chapter includes a way to test a new product without hurting Mother Nature.

In Chapter 4, I discuss ways to save on your energy bill. Using the 8 tips in this chapter, you can save as much as $108.31 monthly. Here's a sneak peek at the strategies:

• Discover the type of lightbulb that will save you nearly $20 a month. And no, it's not fluorescent lighting.

• Learn how one type of curtains and their proper use can reduce your energy bill by $8 a month.

• This unique take on window shutters can help keep the cold out in the winter and the heat out in the summer. Check to see if this is a tip you can use.

If you feel like you're pouring more and more money into your vehicle, you're not alone. In Chapter 5, I will show you 5 ways to save as much as $1,017.82 a month. You'll discover:

• How can you cut your commuting expenses by 75 percent and perhaps get to work more quickly?

• Discover how clicking a car key can save you as much as $7 monthly.

• Learn how to use this often-ignored feature of your car to save money—and help the environment.

In Chapter 6, I will show you how to reduce your monthly clothing budget by $274.91. These 5 tricks will have you rethinking your wardrobe. In this chapter, you'll learn:

• How to calculate cost-per-wear and how it affects the true cost of your clothes.

• How a change in one shopping habit can save you as much as $150 a month.

• 3 easy-to-use tricks to use the next time you wash clothes that will help you last longer.

Chapter 7 is all about saving on entertainment costs. You don't have to pay the exorbitant prices of a movie and accompanying snacks. In this chapter, I discuss 7 ways to save as much as $272.77 a month. Here you'll discover:

• Your secret weapon in savings: the library. Discover all the ways you can save with a free library card.

• How to save nearly $100 monthly on your internet and streaming bill by doing these few easy steps.

• See local theaters and attend concerts for free using this simple tip. (And it doesn't involve anything illegal.)

If you're considering renovating your home or just adding new décor to accent a few words, then chapter 8 is written with you in mind. Here, I show you 6 strategies for saving as much as $235.65 a month in this area. Here's a sneak peek at what you'll find:

• A more than $400 flooring is less expensive than your traditional hardwood floors. And by installing it, you're helping to save the planet.

• 3 ways to save on buying furniture. Use one or all these ways the next time you're looking for new furniture.

• Discover how to brighten your rooms naturally without additional artificial lighting.

Chapter 9 presents 4 ways you can save as much as $97.33 on miscellaneous items. A hodge-podge of strategies you won't want to miss:

• 2 strategies to save on printer ink. You'll be amazed at how easy they are.

• Did you know in the first 3 years of your baby's life, they go through more than 8,000 diapers? You'll want to see this strategy for cutting your expenses for this item by more than $40 a month.

• Discover how your old cellphone can bring you extra money. How did I not know this sooner?

How to Ensure Life-long Habits

The odds are great you won't be able to make all these changes immediately. Change takes time. Establishing a habit takes time.

The best way to ensure your changes become habits is to take one strategy at a time. Implement it. And stick with it for a minimum of three weeks. It's said that your new activity will become second nature to you after that time. Then, you can embrace another new habit.

That's fine, you say, but what about my family? How do I get them to agree to some of these approaches? If helping save the planet doesn't excite your children, then make a game out of the new habit. Have they competed to see who can save the most recyclables or give them stickers when they've taken an environmentally friendly action?

You can get your children excited about these new ways of doing things in many ways. And when they're committed to a project, it'll be hard to stop them.

Read through all the strategies, tips, and tricks I've presented. I've culled them from my ever-growing file and asked people about their favorite ways to save money and help the environment.

Do what you can when you can. Whether you save 50 cents or $5,000, know that your small actions make a difference so we can leave this world a better place.

CHAPTER 1: HOME: 6 WAYS TO SAVE AS MUCH AS $157.03 A MONTH

I have a confession to make. I put them off for far too long when making changes in my household. It's not that I didn't want to save money—or do my part to help the environment.

So, I thought about it. A lot. Then I talked to my family about it. A lot. And then I researched it. Yeah, I did a lot of research.

I hesitated because I thought the changes would

disrupt my family's life. Finally, I committed. I didn't institute all the tips I'd learn in one day. But I introduced them slowly. Once we got used to one new habit, we added another.

If, like me, you're fearful of making wholesale changes in your family's life when it comes to saving money and helping the environment, remember that if you even use one of these tips and suggestions, you've already saved money.

Honestly, though, I discovered the changes didn't bother anyone. In fact, everyone in the household felt empowered that they were making a difference.

CLOTH NAPKINS

Here's a small area where you can save money and feel elegant at the same time: use cloth napkins.

According to a Simmons National Consumer Survey, approximately 11 million Americans used more than six or more packages of paper napkins in 2020, contributing to the 17 million acres of forest cut down yearly.

But here's the catch. Napkins can't be recycled for several reasons. The machines used for this purpose can't handle them. And even if they could, your average paper napkin is made from a low form of paper that can't be reused because the fibers are too short.

By purchasing cloth napkins instead of reusable paper ones, you're doing your part to save trees.

In a year, it's estimated that the average family of four uses 4,380 napkins because each member uses one of their three daily meals. This probably is a conservative number.

This doesn't matter that many times. We'll grab a napkin randomly for those late-night buttery popcorn snacks or other reasons throughout the day.

Costs for paper napkins vary, but I've taken several types from all cost ranges to calculate the average napkin costs approximately $0.0275—or two and three-quarters cents. It's not a large chunk of anyone's budget until you multiply it by the number of napkins used in a year. Then you're spending $120.45.

If you don't have cloth napkins, you'll need to invest.

The average price of a pack of six is roughly $12. Considering that investment, your first year of savings would be $108.45 or $9.04 monthly. In the following years, you'd save $120.45 or $10.04 a month.

PAPER TOWELS

Paper towels are near and dear to my heart—or they were. Their cost seems to rise with every shopping trip. And their math is impossible to figure out. How can eight rolls equal 32? Or does 24 equal 39? And don't even get me started on the pick-your-size. Really?

But they are a necessity. Or were they? When I was trying to find ways to cut my expenses and help the planet, I took a long, hard look at paper towels. And I decided I could do without.

You may want to consider doing without them, too. Some estimates indicate that Americans spend approximately $5.7 billion (billion, with a "b") on paper towels in a single year. The only country that has a nearly equivalent paper towel devotion is France. They spent $635 million (with an "m" million).

How can using cloth towels and rags instead of paper towels help the planet?

There's no way around the fact that the production of paper towels contributes to deforestation. This leads to rising global temperatures, higher greenhouse gas emissions, and habitat loss for many animals.

But that's not all. A paper towel is a single-use item. This means you use them once and toss them. They end up in landfills. You're probably using them daily—perhaps even more than once a day. And you're only one of how many million Americans using them? The waste adds up quickly.

Let's take a quick look at the cost of paper towels. The price of this convenience varies. The most expensive can cost as much as $35 for a dozen rolls, and the least expensive can be purchased for a bit more than $7 for a package of six.

I've taken the average number of paper towels within this price range to be approximately $1.89 per roll. According to many estimates, a family of four uses at least three rolls weekly. That means each week, they use $5.67 worth of towels and in a month, they use $22.68.

If you're willing to give up the convenience, you'll not only help decrease the rate of deforestation, but you'll save $22.68 a month, or $272.16 in a year.

What do you substitute?

You can either create your own rags from old clothing or T-shirts are perfect material. You can also make a one-time purchase of cloth towels designed not only to replace our paper-towel habit but to help the environment as well.

CLEANING SUPPLIES

You don't need to be a germophobe to know that in the average home, germs lurk everywhere. And if you're like me, you'd pay just about any price knowing your family was safe from health hazards. That may be the only reason you tolerate paying the prices on cleaning supplies for your home.

What if I told you there was another way? A way to keep your home clean for less money—and eliminate the health risk many commercial household cleaners hold.

To be fair, most cleaners are safe when used, as the directions on the container indicate. But they do contain potentially hazardous chemicals, mainly if you use several in one cleaning session. If you look at the bottles under your sink right now and read the ingredients, chemicals like ammonia, ethylene glycol, monobutyl acetate (yes, that's one chemical) and sodium hypochlorite pop out at you.

At the very least, some of these can irritate the eyes, nose, and throat. And if you have small children, you're probably worried about the dangers of these cleaners being swallowed accidentally.

But the damage these chemicals do to the environment when they're washed away is incalculable. We wash them down the sink, and they end up in the rivers, streams, and lakes and make their way into the water supply. Their impact doesn't end there, though. Wastewater treatment plants remove only a portion of these chemicals because they don't break down. They stay in the environment and are toxic to the fish and animals in the seas and oceans.

If that weren't enough, add that much of the packaging

isn't recyclable, so they end up sitting in landfills.

But you can save money, improve your family's health, and help save the environment by making your cleaning supplies. And your home will be every bit as clean and sanitized without irritating your eyes, nose, and throat.

It's easier than you think. A simple formula for an all-purpose cleaner is equal parts white vinegar and water plus the rind of a lemon or other citrus fruit for scent. Mix this well and allow it to sit in a glass bottle for a few days before you use it. This is the perfect cleaner to take on mild messes like soap scum.

But there are more on the internet. You can find what you need just for any cleaning occasion.

If you switch out one all-purpose cleaner, you'll save money and help the planet. The average cleaner costs approximately $3.50 for 32 ounces. The exact amount of your vinegar-water spray costs roughly $0.50. If you use one bottle a month, you'll save $3.00, up to $36 a year. That's not counting any other homemade cleaners you might use in addition to this.

REUSABLE WATER BOTTLES

Do you buy bottled water? You're not alone. According to Boston University, one million water bottles are purchased every minute worldwide. That's one million bottles being discarded and ending up in landfills.

Even if you can reduce that waste just a bit, you'd be helping the planet— saving money. Did you know a bottle of water is approximately 2,000 times more expensive than your tap water?

Think about purchasing a stainless-steel bottle. These can last up to a dozen years and cost as low as $15.

Are the savings that much? Surprisingly, they are. According to some statistics, simply by using a refillable bottle for your water consumption, the average American can save about $1,350 in a year. That's a whopping $112.50 in a single month. Who would have thought just a small change could save you so much?

LAWN CARE

If you're like many of us, you probably have a gas-operated lawn mower or have a lawn-care service maintain your lawn, which perhaps uses gas-operated vehicles. And like many of us, you might not have given much thought to the effects these mowers have on the environment.

According to the Environmental Protection Agency, one gas-powered lawn mower produces the same amount of pollution in an hour as a car driven for 45 miles. The truth is "nonroad" engines, including lawn equipment, account for four to five percent of total greenhouse gas emissions in the United States.

But what's the alternative? There are several. The first option is to switch to an electric lawn mower. Sure, you'll have an initial higher cost, but that will eventually pay for itself.

Let's make some quick calculations to help give you an idea of how you can save money. The gas tank of the average push lawn mower holds about a quarter of a gallon. This gives you about half an acre worth of grass cutting. The average gallon of gas is approximately $4, so you're spending $1 on fuel for each quarter acre you cut.

Compare this to electric push mowers that can cut a

half-acre on a single charge. The national average energy price per kWh is approximately $0.14, which is about 3 cents a charge.

So, you can cut your quarter-acre by one and a half cents compared to a dollar. If you cut your lawn once a week, you'd save 6 cents a month or $3.60 a year. While that might not seem like much, you'd also be contributing to a healthier planet.

INSTALL A RAIN BARREL

A rain barrel is an old-fashioned idea that's making a comeback. You install a rain barrel to your gutters (it's easier than you think) and allow the rainwater that lands on your roof to collect in the gutters and ultimately into the barrel. And you have it saved for your outdoor gardening needs.

Before you say this seems like a lot of work, consider this one statistic. During the summer months, lawn and garden irrigation accounts for almost 40 percent of a household's water usage. With a rain barrel, you can collect more water than you might think. According to the Environmental Protection Agency, if the average 2,000-

square-foot house receives an inch of rain during a storm, it can capture more than 500 gallons of water. If you only use a fraction of that water, you'd be helping the environment by reducing your water consumption and saving on your water bill.

Other environmental benefits of rain barrels include a reduction in runoff and pollution, as well as a reduction in erosion. Moreover, the use of rain barrels helps reduce flooding and helps to lessen sewer backups.

According to a national survey conducted by the DC Urban Gardeners, the use of a rain barrel reduced water bills by approximately $35 a month during the summer. That's $105 for the three-month season. If you spread those savings throughout the year, it would average out to $8.75 a month.

Even More Ways to Save

The following tips can save you money. But it's difficult to estimate just how much money a month you'll gain. So, while I can't include these in your overall monthly savings for the home, rest assured your wallet will thank you if you give any of these a try. And yes, the environment will also thank you.

TRY XERISCAPING

Don't you want to mow the lawn at all?

Do I have an idea for you! It's called xeriscaping, and while it sounds like some weird escape room game, it's, in fact, a landscaping concept that's proving popular—especially in arid areas.

It's also considered an irrigation process that eliminates the need to water your lawn. You'll replace your grass with a variety of plants that thrive in a dry region. Some individuals believe this concept can reduce water use by between 50 and 75 percent. Quite savings.

Popularized by the Denver, Colorado water department, xeriscaping has 7 principles:

1. Planning and Design

Before you even begin to plant a tree, you should plan the area's design to be landscaped. Part of the plan is to incorporate the maximum savings of water through properly selecting plants.

2. Soil Improvements

In a xeriscape, the soil type is either clay or sand. Soil composed of sand doesn't hold water well and typically requires more irrigation. Clay soil, on the other hand, retains water well but doesn't dry out as quickly as sandy soil.

3. Efficient irrigation

Xeriscaping promotes efficient watering of foliage, such as infrequent and deep watering, which helps the growth of deep roots. You can experience an even more significant saving on water consumption by adjusting the automatic sprinkling systems with the seasons.

4. Plant zones

You can minimize water waste by planting strategically, that is, by grouping greenery dependent on sunlight and moisture needs together.

5. Make use of mulches

The use of mulch helps to minimize moisture evaporation. It prevents soil and plant roots from drying out. While both the organic and inorganic types are effective, their placement is what counts. Effectiveness depends more on the direction the landscape is facing the sun.

6. Turf alternatives

Xeriscaping perfectly uses low-water-use turfs, like buffalo and blue grama grass.

7. Maintenance

This type of garden is also typically less maintenance than traditional landscaping.

Okay, I save on water, but are there any other benefits to changing my yard? Why yes, there are. Recent studies show that when xeriscaping is done correctly, it can reduce the cooling requirements of a home by up to 45 percent. This could translate into thousands of dollars on your energy bill in just one year.

Because xeriscaping is low maintenance, you'll be spending less on plants, seeds, fertilizer, and pest control, to name a few of the costs of traditional landscaping.

If you're looking for another incentive to change your yard, you may want to check out some of the rebate programs offered to homeowners.

Keep in mind you don't have to xeriscape your entire yard. You can do a portion of it, and you'll still be saving money.

INSTALL A BIDET

Every day, more than 27,000 trees are felled to stock the world's bathrooms with toilet paper. That means approximately 12 million trees are cut down every single year. You can lessen your dependency on toilet paper and help the environment by installing a bidet.

Popular in Europe, a bidet attaches to your toilet and spritzed water to clean your backside. While you'll use more water this way, you will reduce your use of toilet paper. Some individuals use 80 percent less toilet paper with their bidet.

USE A TOASTER OVEN

Not every meal requires the use of the oven. This is

especially true if you only cook for one or two individuals. This marvelous small appliance is perfect for this mission. More cost-effective than your oven, the average toaster oven uses only 12 to 13 percent of the power of the full-size appliance.

If you use every one of these strategies, you can save up to $157.03 a month. But even by using one or two of these tips, you can still save a portion of this amount. Use any of these tips that would fit your family life, and know that when you do, you're contributing to helping the environment.

In the next chapter, we will discuss strategies to help you lower your food costs. You'll be amazed at the many options available that will help the health of our planet, too.

Chapter 2: Food And Grocery: 6 Ways to Save as Much as $316 per Month

Who hasn't complained about the price of groceries?

We all need to eat. That means we're buying groceries more often than we care about and spending more money than we can afford to.

What if I told you there were some strategies you could use on your next grocery trip that could save you money? And if you used these regularly, could you rack up a sizable savings every month?

Interested? I knew you would be.

REUSABLE COFFEE PODS

Single-use coffee pods are more popular than ever. Nearly 16 million households drink their coffee brewed through this way accounting for a $5 billion industry.

There's a good reason for their popularity. In addition to making a good cup of coffee, they make it unnecessary to make a full pot for only a cup of two. So, you're saving water in addition to coffee. But they were expensive. The average price of a pound of coffee breaks down to less than 20 cents a cup compared to 74 cents for a K-cup.

And they're not the most environmentally friendly items. While these pods can be recycled, it takes extra effort on your part. Keurig does offer recycling, but it costs. What's an environmentally conscious coffee lover to do?

Buy a reusable K-cup. A one-time cup purchase will allow you to fill it again and again with the ground coffee of your choice. Let's say you have two coffee drinkers in your household. You could save up to $400 a year, or approximately $33 a month, without forgetting the caffeine.

MEAL PLANNING

Planning your meals ahead of time and buying accordingly will not only save you money, but some experts believe it's the "single-most powerful" action you can take to help reduce your carbon footprint.

Families who plan meals a week or a month at a time find they make fewer trips to the store (which means less gasoline and emissions), spend less on food, and, most notably for the environment, waste less food.

You probably haven't given much thought about how throwing away uneaten food affects the environment. Leftover food is inevitable. We've all thrown out vegetables past their prime or foods with use-by dates that have expired.

A vast number of natural resources and energy go into growing, processing, and eventually throwing away all that wasted food. At every stage of the food system, we create greenhouse gases that pollute the atmosphere, destabilize the climate, and deplete our increasingly scarce fresh water and fertile soils.

Much of the wasted food eventually finds its way to landfills, where it generates methane, the greenhouse gas more than 86 times more powerful than carbon dioxide. These global landfill emissions are estimated to comprise approximately 17 percent of all methane emissions. This makes it the third largest human source of gas.

In the United States alone, the Environmental Protection Agency estimates that eliminating food waste would have the same positive impact as taking one-quarter of all the cars in the U.S. off the road.

FOOD WASTE STRATEGY

When you plan your meals ahead of time, you're only buying the food you need for the week and then preparing them according to your plan. When you keep to the plan, all the food gets used. You don't find that bunch of broccolis in the back of the fridge that's a month old. When planning your meals, you're making a family food-waste reduction strategy.

Meal planning saves you money. You're not buying those unnecessary groceries, and you're only grocery shopping once a week. No dash-in shopping trips to buy that one thing you need for supper tonight.

Experts have estimated that overall, families have saved about $1,500, a conservative estimate. That comes to about $125 a month.

If you're interested in planning your meal, the internet has many good sites and blogs to help you get started.

BRING YOUR BAG

Consider this: the average plastic grocery bag is used for 12 minutes. After that, the bag has served its purpose and becomes a waste. And the environmental footprint of these bags is large. Some 30 billion plastic bags are used in the U.S. alone each year. Their production takes up 8 percent of the world's total oil production to make the plastic and another 12 million barrels of oil to manufacture the bags.

I love saving the planet, but can I save money by bringing reusable bags?

The answer is yes. Many grocery stores will give you a discount for using your bags. You'll want to ask. The discount is about five cents for each bag saved. If you use five bags each week, you'll save 25 cents a week or $1.00 a month and $12 in a year. And Mother Earth will thank you.

BUY IN BULK

Do you think only large families buy in bulk? Think again. You can save money—and help the environment—by buying in bulk, even if your family is small. Let's start with this fact: some experts estimate that 15 percent of the cost of that box of cereal at your grocery store is due to packaging. You're paying for something that ultimately gets thrown away and languishes in a landfill.

You don't have to look too closely at your grocer's shelf to notice most individual products are packaged in plastic. Not only does the packaging contribute to a higher price, but it also contains chemicals hazardous to the water and soil that harm the environment and, in turn, the food chain.

But that's only the start. You automatically use fewer

plastic grocery bags when you buy in larger quantities. We've mentioned that Americans alone use 30 billion bags a year. Even if you can help reduce that astounding number a tiny bit, you'll be helping the environment.

Another compelling reason to consider buying in bulk is the fewer trips to the store, which means using less gasoline, reducing your personal fuel budget and helping the environment with a reduction in carbon dioxide emissions.

If you intend to try this money-saving strategy, you'll naturally want to start with the typical bulk items: grains, nuts, spices, dried fruit, and cereal legumes. You can bring your containers for these or fill a paper bag. You then pay according to the weight of the product.

But don't stop there. Other products can be bought in large quantities—if you have room for them. Think toilet paper, paper towels, and cleaning products (that is, if you haven't already changed over to more eco-friendly products).

How much can you save by buying in bulk? That depends on your buying habits and the size of your family, of course, but some statistics suggest that some families can save more than $1,000 a year by shopping this way. This saves you $83 a month. That's no small change.

BULK BUYING TIPS

Are you thinking about buying in bulk but not sure how to go about it? No worries. I've included several tips to help you get started on the right foot so you can make it a lifelong habit.

1. Prepare ahead of time.

You'll want to find a storage area for your purchases. This could mean you dedicate a part of your kitchen pantry to food or several shelves in your garage or basement for nonperishables, like toilet paper and paper towels.

In addition to this, though, you may need to gather containers for your purchases. Think about glass jars for the dry goods or some other smaller container that allows you easy access to them.

2. Combine your purchases with others.

Think about going in with a family member or a

neighbor and buying the products together to get even greater savings.

3. Pay close attention to self-life.

One word of caution: you can overstock your pantry. Don't buy so much that the product expires or goes bad before you can use it. Certain products have a shorter shelf-life than others. You'll want to be aware of that as you make your purchases.

Shop Online

The delivery of groceries hit peak popularity during the Covid years. The pandemic restricted our movements (for fear of contracting a potentially deadly virus). Perhaps you used this service. Despite the occasional fees and the custom of tipping your shopper, you can still save money by using this service. And on top of that, you're helping the environment because you're not driving to the grocery store regularly.

It's convenient. Undoubtedly, the convenience of online shopping is one of the major advantages. It saves you time—and they say time is money. Instead of spending an hour at the grocery store, you can spend that hour with your family. Or if you work from home, you can hit double savings. You can continue to work while the groceries get bought and delivered.

It stops impulse purchases. When you create your list for the online service, you're far less likely to make an impulse purchase. It's easier to get caught up with the delicious-looking quart of ice cream or that irresistible pastry when you see it in person—and smell it. This one aspect of online shopping can result in long-term significant savings. This is especially true if you take your children shopping. Children are the best (or worse) impulse shoppers.

Online shopping helps the environment. You may not feel as if your weekly shopping trip hurts the environment. But consider that just about every other family is doing the same thing. The harm in the form of pollution and other irritants adds up. Quickly.

At least that's the conclusion of a recent United States Department of Agriculture survey discovered recently. It learned that 88 percent of American households drive to the store to buy groceries. The average trip is four miles.

It is estimated that if these families limited their trips to once a week, the roundtrips would add up to a whopping 42 billion miles.

It's projected that in addition to helping the planet, the average family can save $12 a month on gas by shopping online. That's not even counting the potential savings of the groceries themselves.

If you decide to try online grocery shopping, you'll want to follow a few strategies to ensure you enjoy the best possible savings. First and foremost, you'll want to compare prices. Of course, you'll want to compare the cost of groceries, but you'll also want to research online services. Some of these services are offered by various stores. Others, like Instacart, are independent of any retailer.

Just like if you were doing in-person shopping, you'd want to be aware of retail promotions and other discounts available for online purchases.

For items you use frequently, consider subscriptions. This way of shopping typically provides lower prices or discounts, helping you to save even more money.

How much money can you save on online grocery shopping? There's no way I can accurately estimate the savings on groceries for your family. There are just far too many factors. But I can tell you that if you're the average family, you can save a minimum of $12 a month on gasoline for your car alone.

Vacuum Seal Foods

I know. This tip requires the purchase of an appliance. But vacuum sales only cost about $100 these days. If you don't already own one, this purchase will pay for itself in the first month and a half of use.

The concept of vacuum sealing is that it removes the air from a package before sealing it with heat. The removal of the air slows the oxidation process, which contributes to food spoilage—and prevents the growth of bacteria and mold while helping to preserve the freshness and flavor of the food. And, yes, it also helps save its nutritional contents.

Perhaps the biggest benefit to your budget is that vacuum sealing an item extends its shelf-life. Most food lasts three to five times longer with this method than in plastic containers or plastic zipper bags. Doing that also helps reduce the amount of food you throw out. Reduced waste means less environmental impact, including fewer greenhouse gas emissions.

I know what you're thinking: The plastic bags the food gets sealed in can't be good for the environment. You can reuse these bags simply by washing them out. In the end, you'll be using fewer bags than had you stored your food in the single-use zipper bags.

It's said the average American family wastes roughly a quarter of the food and beverages it buys in a year, or roughly $1,500. If you could save even half of that—say $750 in a year—that monthly savings would still be substantial, about $62.

TIPS TO SAVE EVEN MORE

The tips above are only the tip of the iceberg when it comes to spending less on food. There are more tips that you might be able to use, but I can't accurately estimate the monthly savings for them.

The only way to know how much you can save is by

trying them out. You've got nothing to lose and potentially quite a bit of money—along with the environment—to save.

1. Grow your own herbs.

How many times do you buy a package of fresh herbs on your trips to the store? Each package is about $2 or $3 if I use herbs regularly, as I do, that adds up. Fast.

But have you ever considered growing your own herbs? You don't need a yard, and truthfully, you don't even need a green thumb. Herbs are among the easiest plants to grow. You can grow them on your kitchen windowsill. They'll thrive.

You can begin by buying the plants themselves or purchasing seeds and watching them grow. The good news is that these plants last all year long and, in some cases, will keep growing for multiple years.

The average cost of five herbal plants is approximately $19. That's a one-time purchase for the year. You could save even more money if you decided to grow your herbs from seeds. Five packets of seeds would cost you approximately $8. Again, that's the sum total of your herbal purchases for an entire year.

2. Buy seasonal produce locally.

When you buy produce from local farmers, you reduce your carbon footprint, help a small local business, and save money. And, yes, getting fresher, more delicious fruits and vegetables. You'll benefit not only from the taste, but you'll notice the produce lasts longer. This reduces waste. Buying locally also means less plastic packaging.

3. Enjoy a meatless meal occasionally.

No, you don't need to become a vegan or even a vegetarian but having a meatless meal once a week can cut down on your grocery bill. Meat is expensive. If you can, substitute it with an omelet for dinner or even cheese (like a cheese pizza) or beans and pasta. You'll still get the protein your body needs, but you'll be spending less. You'll also be helping the environment. Did you know that at least 25% and as much as 34% of global greenhouse gas emissions are caused by food production and animal waste. One meatless meal a day can help reduce those statistics—even a little.

If you decided to use all the strategies in this chapter you could save as much as $316 a month on your grocery bill. It seems incredible that these six small changes could help reduce your food budget by that much.

Even if you can't implement them all, by using just one or two of these, you'd be able to see savings. Don't be afraid to try them at least once. Maybe the strategy won't work for your family, but maybe it will. That's the fun of trying new things. And who knows? You may find another way to contribute to the good of the environment.

In the next chapter, I will show you strategies for saving money on body and beauty products while helping the planet.

Chapter 3: Body and Beauty: 6 Ways to Save as Much as $39.04 per Month

You don't have to be a fashionista to use body and beauty products. We use them every day. That makes it a massive market. In fact, it's a $48.8 billion market and is only poised for more growth.

It's estimated the average woman spends more than $800 a year on body and beauty products, while the average male spends more than $500. Products like shampoo and conditioner, soaps, body lotions, and cosmetics take a chunk out of the average American family's budget.

From the packaging, which amounts to 120 billion units of trash yearly, to the demand for oils for the products themselves, stripping our habitats, beauty products are major sources of damage to the planet.

But that doesn't mean there aren't strategies you can use to help reduce your beauty-related costs and help contribute to helping the environment.

SHAMPOO BARS

Approximately nine million tons of plastic are thrown into the ocean each year. That's the equivalent of one garbage truck of plastic dumped into the sea every minute. Several of your bottles of shampoo are undoubtedly included.

You can help reduce the amount of plastic tossed and save money by switching to shampoo bars. Much as the name implies, a shampoo bar is a shampoo that is greatly concentrated and formed into a bar. It is a solid form of traditional shampoo. So, what's the difference? Shampoo bars don't include the water that the liquid versions use. You must supply that. And many don't contain the detergents you often find in other shampoos.

Oh, yes, and there's one other thing lacking in a shampoo bar—the plastic bottle.

If you're wondering how washing your hair with a bar would work, well, it's quite easy. If you wet your hair like you usually do, then you have two choices. You can rub the bar directly onto your hair and scalp until it leathers, then massage your scalp. Your other option is to rub the bar into your hands like you would a bar of soap, then apply it to your scalp with your hands. When you're done, you rinse.

And yes, there is such a thing as a conditioner bar. You can also use the bar version if you use a hair conditioner. And you'd use it the same way as the shampoo.

This highly concentrated shampoo version, meaning

one bar can be used for more washes than the liquid alternative. The cost of a shampoo bar is approximately $15. This is the same as buying three to four bottles of liquid shampoo. The amount you save varies, depending on the type of shampoo you use and how much you use. But it's estimated you can save as much as $60 a year just by using bar shampoo. That's a monthly savings of $5.

REFILLABLE CONTAINERS

If you're not quite ready to make the jump to bar shampoo, that's understandable. But you can save money and help the environment by switching to refillable beauty products.

The beauty industry is stepping up to provide its customers with sustainable packaging and the option of purchasing refills instead of buying new products in new packaging. And we're not just talking shampoo, though that's one of your options. These days, you can get just about any beauty product, from fragrances to makeup, in refillable containers.

And the refills are less expensive since you're not paying for the original packaging.

The use of refillable products has the potential, according to environmentalists, to reduce carbon dioxide production by 70 percent and use 45 percent less water than using disposable containers.

Depending on the products you buy and the frequency you use them, you may be able to save $110 or more a year. That's a bit more than $9 a month.

Washable Cotton Rounds

Where would the history of the beauty industry be without the cotton ball? We've all used them for a variety of reasons. And then we toss them. You can immediately see the problem. We only use them once. We throw them away. Wasteful, right? Not only does this cost you money, it also hurts the environment. All those cotton balls eventually end up in a landfill.

Not only do they end up hurting the planet, but their creation also damages the earth. They take a considerable amount of water to make these.

Now you have the opportunity not only to help Mother Earth but also to increase your budget by using washable cotton rounds instead. They can be used for all the tasks you use the disposable ones for. You can find these made of bamboo hemp or even organic cotton.

If you opt for the organic cotton variety, you'll be purchasing a product that uses 88 percent less water and takes 62 percent less energy to make than the single-use variety. And it contains no harsh chemicals.

The initial cost of the reusable type will be higher. You can buy a bag of 100 cotton balls for about $4. A set of reusable cotton rounds will cost you about $4.50 for 80. But wait. The average family buys nine packages of cotton balls a year, amounting to $45. But you'll only need this one package of reusable rounds for the year. You've saved $40.50 in a year or $3.37 a month.

SUBSCRIPTION BOXES

If you've never joined a beauty subscription box service before, perhaps this is the time to consider it. The service ships you regularly, typically monthly, various beauty products. You can customize the box to include your favorite and most needed products, but you'll also discover some surprises when you open the package.

You pay a flat monthly fee for this service, which can vary from as little as $10 to $15 per month to $20 to $25, depending on how much it holds. And yes, you can get monthly subscriptions that cost as much as $75.

Regardless of the plan you choose, one thing is sure. You'll be paying less overall for the products than if you had purchased them separately.

Some boxes that cost $10 have an upward $50 worth of products. But let's be conservative here and say your $10 subscription yields only $20 worth of products. In this case, you save $10 a month on your beauty regimen through this one change in lifestyle.

And, of course, don't forget you won't be running out of cosmetics; they'll be coming to you. That helps reduce your carbon footprint.

MAKE YOUR OWN

Yes, it is possible to make your beauty products. From soap to lip balm, many eco-conscious individuals who want to save money have discovered that homemade products are as effective as commercially purchased items. And they come with fewer side effects.

Making your beauty products is a win for the planet, too. Let's face it: there's always that portion of the product at the bottom of the bottle that you can't get out, regardless of how hard you try. And sometimes, it's a sizeable amount. You won't have that problem with your homemade products.

You'll also be using less packaging overall when you make your products. The best types of containers are amber glass bottles. They're reusable and protect against light degradation. And, oh, yeah, they're recyclable.

If that isn't enough to at least get you thinking about making your beauty products, consider this. Making your products means you know precisely what they have in them—and what they don't. They won't have preservatives or chemicals that fill the commercial products. But they may have ingredients like sweet almond oil, organic cocoa butter, and natural aloe vera gel. You get the picture.

How much can you save?

Your total savings depend on the number of products

you make as well as the amount you need. But overall, you will be able to save money. Here are some examples:

Body lotion. Commercially made body lotion costs approximately $6.00 for 12 ounces anywhere. Of course, you can buy specialty types for more. But for our purposes, this is a great comparison price. If you make body lotion at home, the cost will average about $4 for the same amount.

Exfoliating hand scrub. The cheapest I can find this product is for $6 for 16 ounces. Many are priced twice that and more. But you can make the same amount for half that at about $3.

Let's say you use one bottle of each of these products monthly. Your savings? $5 for one month or $60 yearly.

USING A REUSABLE TISSUE PACK

How many tissues does your family use? According to research conducted by the manufacturer of Kleenex brand tissues, there are always four boxes in various rooms. Homeowners buy tissues about eight times a year. In one year, based on these statistics, the average family uses 32 boxes of tissues.

Some households use more. Your family may use less. However, when you add these numbers up, it comes to more than 255 billion used in the United States alone in a year. And that number is only expected to grow.

Environmentally, this demand has damaged forests like those in Canada, where one million acres are lost yearly to meet the U.S.'s paper demands. In the Canadian boreal forest alone, logging to satisfy the need for paper goods is responsible for 26 metric tons of carbon dioxide yearly. That's the same amount as adding 5.5 million cars on the road.

What's the alternative? I'm glad you asked. You can purchase a reusable pack of tissues. It comes with an environmentally friendly, washable case and six cotton tissues. The case has a barrier that separates the used tissues from the clean. You use one, put it aside. When you've gone through the entire pack, you wash them. They can be washed and reused up to 520 times.

That's great, but will it save me money? Yes, it will. Let's say you live in a household that uses 32 boxes of tissues a year, as described above. $2.50 a box amounts to a yearly tissue budget of $80. One reusable pack costs about $24 and will last much longer than a year. You've saved $56 or $4.67 a month in the first year of use alone. In the second year of use, you'd save $80 because you do not need to buy disposable tissues. And that adds up to $6.67 a month.

MORE WAYS TO SAVE MONEY

But wait…there's more. You can use other methods to save money on your toiletries and beauty products. They're just a bit more challenging to calculate how much the average family would save. But save they would. With that in mind, here are a few more tips for getting the most for your money and contributing to the good of the planet.

1. Virtual samples

The Travel-size cosmetics samples have been a staple of the industry for probably forever. It's a quick and easy marketing strategy for businesses to give you several in hopes that you'll love the free sample so much that you'll buy the full-size version.

You've probably never realized that those small bottles

present problems for recycling companies. And maybe not in the way you might think. The tester bottles, as they're called, are so small that the recycling machines can't use them. They're sorted and sent directly to a landfill despite your best efforts at recycling.

But wait, there's more. You need to apply that lipstick, nail polish, or foundation somehow. This usually involves a cotton pad or other disposable product, which introduces another source of pollution.

And up until recently, there wasn't much you could do about it.

Enter virtual samples, a method of seeing how the cosmetics look on you without the packaging and the cotton rounds. The development of this system was accelerated due to the constraints of the pandemic. Using smart mirrors in brick-and-mortar stores or apps is an eco-friendly way of sampling products.

And, with the growth of online consultation services, you don't need to leave the comfort of your home. You can speak to an advisor in many cases, who'll guide you through the process. They can answer your questions and even give you recommendations about the products.

The bonus of in-home shopping? You don't have to use your vehicle to find your next favorite eyeliner. The environment will thank you for that.

I can't tell you how much you'll save a month using virtual cosmetic samples. That depends on your lifestyle, the makeup you wear, and the number of physical samples you pick up while shopping.

2. Reusable razor

Disposable razors are convenient, and they're designed to be colorfully attractive. But they aren't environmentally friendly. Most of the razors are not biodegradable. This leads to literally billions of hazardous wastes in landfills—yearly. The blades eventually rust away, leaving the plastic handles and causing them to sit for years if not decades.

A reusable metal razor is an environmentally friendly option that, in the long run, will also save you money. One razor can last for years. The initial cost of the reusable version is more than a disposable, but you're not buying one every couple of months.

Following all the strategies in this chapter could save

as much as $39.04 a month. While that may not seem like a lot, in a year, it adds up to $468.48 a year. That's a nice amount of money that can go toward your dreams.

In the next chapter, I'm showing you strategies for reducing your energy usage, which will not only reduce your monthly bill but help contribute to the good of the planet.

Chapter 4: Energy: 8 Ways to Save as Much to $108.31 per Month

Studies show that, on average, 35 percent of the energy you use in your home is wasted. That's right. You're paying for it, but it isn't helping you wash your clothes or dry your dishes, or, most importantly, it isn't keeping you warm.

But it's costing you money. It's said that the average home energy bill is $117 a month. If the studies are correct, you're paying $40.95 monthly and getting nothing to show for it. Not only that, but the wasted energy affects the environment. Coal is the second most used fossil fuel to generate electricity in the United States.

It's composed mainly of organic carbon, is crushed into a fine powder, and then heated to produce electricity. This process causes the release of carbon emissions and contributes to the greenhouse effect.

However, you can increase the efficiency of your energy consumption and help lower carbon emissions. And don't worry. I'm not suggesting you turn your thermostat down to 64 degrees or use candlelight to read.

The truth is that with a few minor changes in your habits and the products you use, you can reduce your electric bill. While it might not be able to reduce your usage by a full 35 percent that's said to be wasted, you can see significant savings. And the environment will be grateful.

LED LIGHTING

The cost of lighting the house accounts for approximately 15 percent of the average homeowner's electric bill. What if I told you it is possible to reduce your lighting costs even more? And it's as simple as the type of bulb you use.

It's true. By switching your current incandescent or fluorescent lights for LED—light-emitting diodes—you can reduce your electric bill and help the planet in the process. The latest generation of LED lights uses up to 90 percent energy and lasts 25 times longer than your current bulbs.

While you're reducing your energy costs with LED lighting, you're also helping the planet in three ways. First, using less energy means the demand for power plants is also reduced, decreasing greenhouse gas emissions. Secondly, LED lights contain no toxic elements. By contrast, fluorescent strip lights contain mercury, among other noxious chemicals, that contaminate the environment when dumped into a landfill.

Finally, their longer lifespan means lower carbon emissions. The need for fewer lights translates into the use of fewer resources involved in the manufacturing processes, including packing materials and transportation.

Admittedly, the cost of purchasing LED lights is more than incandescent or fluorescent, but the savings in the long run make these lights so appealing. The average homeowner will save $225 a year by using these lights. That's $18.75 a month. That will surely brighten your day.

Turn Down the Water Heater

We all love our hot showers and baths. It's a luxury that we can't seem to do without. So, you may balk at the idea of fooling with your relaxing shower. But simply turning the heat from 140 degrees Fahrenheit to 120 can help you save on your energy costs.

The truth is that gas boilers that give us hot water use more energy and create more greenhouse gas emissions than any other home appliance. We don't notice it because we don't see the water heater. We only feel its effects.

The average family can save nearly $145 a year simply by decreasing their water temperature by 20 degrees. This results in a $12 monthly savings. And you're helping the planet—that's priceless.

PROGRAM YOUR THERMOSTAT

Do you have a programmable thermostat? Do you use it? If you have one, you can save on energy costs simply by letting it do its thing. If you don't have one, you may want to consider one.

It's a simple and painless area where you can save money and help save the planet. Set the thermostat to adjust the temperature automatically when you're away from the house or sleep. The average consumer saves about 8 percent on energy costs by doing this. That's approximately $50 a year or $4.17 a month.

You'll also contribute to reducing greenhouse gas emissions and fighting climate change.

ENERGY-EFFICIENT CURTAINS

Did you know you can save as much as 7 percent on your energy expenses simply by switching to energy-efficient curtains? It's one of the most effective ways to lower your energy costs.

The windows account for up to 30 percent of heat loss

in an average home. That means one-third of your heat is escaping through the windows. In the summer, experts estimate that 76 percent of the sunlight that hits the windows enters the house as heat. This causes your air conditioner to work longer and harder, increasing your energy bill.

That's where energy-efficient curtains can help. They're thick, heavy curtains that have a layer of acrylic foam on one side to provide insulation to help reduce the amount of heat and air entering or leaving through the windows.

Essentially, they create a barrier against air transfer through your home's windows.

The key to their efficiency lies in their proper use. The U.S. Department of Energy estimates that 75 percent of residential window coverings remain in the same position daily. They're either always open or permanently closed.

To help reduce your heating bill in winter, you should open your curtains on a sunny morning. This is especially true of those that receive direct sunlight. This helps to heat your home all day long.

But when night falls, it's best to close all the curtains.

This helps to prevent heat loss.

That's the winter strategy. You'll use curtains differently in the summer. Keep the curtains that aren't facing the sun open. This helps you to avoid turning on lights. You'll want to close curtains facing the sun to prevent the sun from heating the room.

Regardless of how you use your new energy-efficient curtains, you'll want the thermal backing to be white or a light color to reflect the light which will help to lower your energy bill even more.

So how much can you save?

I mentioned you can save up to 7 percent on your energy bill by using these curtains properly. It's estimated the average monthly electric bill is $117. Seven percent of that is approximately $8.19. Your savings may be even more, depending on your expenses.

And don't forget you're reducing your carbon footprint using less energy. So, it's a win for both your wallet and Mother Nature.

SMART POWER STRIPS

Many electronics in your home use electricity, whether they are turned on or not. When your computer goes to "sleep," it's still using electricity. This unseen energy drain is called "vampire load." And it's silently costing you money. Sometimes, it accounts for up to 10 percent of your energy. But now you can fight back.

No doubt, you're already familiar with the power strip. The device has a base that holds multiple outlets and has an on-and-off switch. Many also come with a built-in circuit breaker. At one end of the power strip is a cord so you can plug it in.

They're a great convenience since our homes seem to have more electronic appliances than ever before. But they're not necessarily energy efficient. If the appliance is plugged into the power strip—they still use energy.

But there's now a better, more cost-efficient item on the market. It's called the smart power strip and can turn off the electricity to the electronic gadgets when it senses they're not in use. Some now include USB ports as well, allowing you to free up your other outlets for standard plugs. The criteria for shutting down the device vary depending on your chosen type. Here are three of the most common:

Timer-equipped. This is for devices that are used according to a predictable routine. They're used at a specific time of the day and at a particular length. It's convenient to save energy by not having the device on when not in use.

Occupancy-sensing. This variety has a sensor that detects movement in a room. It will turn off the device if it senses no one is in the room. When a person walks into the room, it can sense that and turn the device on. Many of these also allow you to program how long it waits to turn the device off. In this way, if you leave a room only to return in a short while, it won't turn everything off.

Current sensing. One type of power strip can detect when the current drops on a device. When the device switches off or enters sleep mode, it turns the power off. The power will be turned back once the device is turned on again.

How much can you save by using these power strips?

These power strips can reduce and even eliminate vampire load in many cases. If the average monthly home energy bill is $117, then a 10-percent saving is $11.70 monthly. Or $140.40 a year. And you're reducing your carbon footprint.

TAKE SHORTER SHOWERS

We all love that long invigorating shower. But it also wastes water. It may not seem like a lot, but the amount of wasted water increases daily, month after month. If you can manage to get in and out of the shower faster, you will save money and be conserving water and doing your part to save the planet.

Shortening your shower by only four minutes can save up to 4,000 gallons of water annually. That translates into $100 yearly savings or approximately $8.34 a month.

USE THAT DISHWASHER

Excuse me? Did you say I should run my dishwasher?

Yes, I did. The research is clear on this one. Washing dishes in the appliance as compared to hand washing the plates and utensils saves you money—and helps the planet.

Let's break down this tip so you can see the difference. The most efficient Energy-Star dishwashers use approximately 3.5 gallons of water for each cycle. Older ones use up to three times 10 to 15 gallons a cycle.

Kitchen faucets use 1.5 to 2 gallons of water every minute, which means washing the family's dishes expends anywhere between 9 to 27 gallons. Of course, this will vary depending on how you wash and rinse your dishes.

To get the most energy savings from the dishwasher, you should always wait until you have a full load to use it. This gets the most efficiency from the electricity and hot water used to run it. And if you want to go that extra mile in savings, omit the heated dry cycle. The water in most dishwashers is generally hot enough to evaporate on its own once the door is open.

The EPA has crunched the numbers for you on this tip. Running a full dishwasher instead of washing your dishes by hand can save up to $465 a year on combined water and energy bills. That's an average monthly savings of $38.75.

Don't you have a dishwasher? Consider buying one if you can afford it. It's said the average cost of one is approximately $970. The appliance would pay for itself in two years.

DRY YOUR CLOTHES OUTSIDE

If you just forgot you had a clothes dryer and used a clothesline instead, you'd be helping the environment and saving some money. Environmental experts estimate clothes dryers—residential, commercial, and industrial—account for 15 to 20 percent of all domestic energy use in the United States. These appliances in 2007, one single year, produced 54.72 million metric tons of CO_2, the greenhouse-producing gas.

On a family level, the Department of Energy estimates that the clothes dryer alone accounts for 5.8 percent of your electric bill. Every time you dry a load of clothes, it costs you about 30 to 40 cents if you have an electric dryer. If your appliance is powered by gas, it costs about 15 to 20 cents a load.

Over the course of 18 years—the length of time an average dryer lasts—this appliance costs about $1,500 to operate. While that doesn't sound like much, it breaks down to $83.34 yearly or $6.94 monthly. By drying your clothes, you'd be saving that every month.

Why, yes, I know that one drawback to drying clothes outside or on a folding table is that they're stiff. But did you know that adding half a cup of vinegar to your machine's rinse cycle will help soften them? And you won't need to buy any fabric softener.

More Ways to Save Even More

I've included a few more strategies you can use to slash your energy bill even more. These tips, though, aren't easily calculated to show how much money you can save. The variables here depend on your situation. But two things are certain: you will reduce your energy bill and help the environment.

1. Replace your showerhead.

If your showerhead is old—and by old, I mean it's from the 1990s—then replacing it with a new one will automatically slash the water you use in the shower by nearly half.

Older high-flow showerheads can use as much as 5.5 gallons of water every minute. Take a five-minute shower, and you've got 27.5 gallons. Low-flow showers, by contrast, use a maximum of 2.5 gallons a minute. That five-minute shower now only used 12.5 gallons. You've saved 15 gallons of water with only one shower. Multiply that by the number of showers that get taken in your household daily, and the savings add up even faster.

Using less water means a lower energy bill and a better environment.

2. Use that ceiling fan.

A ceiling fan is more than a pretty accent to your room. It can help lower cool your home in the summer. The key is to use it in conjunction with your air conditioner. This fan can cool a room by about 4 degrees, which may seem like little. But you can turn the air conditioner down. The fan uses less energy than the air conditioner.

3. Shutter your windows.

Window shutters make every house look a bit cozier. Well, they also help save you energy. This is especially true if you put them inside your windows. That's right. It may sound a bit unconventional if you're used to seeing them outside of homes. By installing them inside, you can use them easily whenever you need them. They could block a lot of cold air or even hot air, especially if your windows are older and let air in. The only drawback to them is that they need quite a bit of room on either side of the window. They look cute, they save you energy, and they help the environment—the trifecta of energy savings.

If you use all eight of the strategies presented in this chapter, you can save up to $108.67 a month on your energy bill. That's an astounding $1,304.04 a year. Even a fraction of those savings will help your budget and, yes, help the planet. And I haven't even counted on the extra hints that I can't give you an estimate for.

Ready for even more savings? Then follow me to the next chapter, where I will show you ways you can snip the expenses on transportation.

Chapter 5: Transportation: 5 Ways to Save as Much as $1,017.82 per Month

The statistics don't lie. Our cars cost us money. But for many of us, it's our sole means of commuting to work, getting groceries, and getting the kids to their activities. In many cities, public transportation isn't a viable option.

The cost of owning a car is quite staggering when you add up all the expenses. And the automobile club, AAA, has done that for us. The organization estimates it costs us, on average, $8,558 a year just to own and operate one vehicle. Approximately $1,267 of that amount goes to filling the car with gas, another $1,222 is taken by insurance, and maintenance costs run about $792. The rest of the expenses go to finance charges, depreciation, license and registration fees and taxes, as well as the cost of tires.

Then there's the monthly car payments. The average monthly payment for a new car is more than $500.

I don't mean to be the bearer of worse news, but our cars also create a sizable carbon footprint. The vehicles make up fifty-five percent of a typical family's carbon footprint.

That doesn't mean, however, that we can't find ways not only to help us save money in transportation but also help the environment.

Let's look at some ways we can help our budget and the environment at the same time.

Take the Bus or Subway

Public transportation is a practical first step to saving

money and the planet if it's available in your area. You may be surprised at just how much money can be saved by commuting to work. According to a recent American Public Transportation Association report, the average person can save up to $9,515 a year in gas expenses just by taking the bus or subway. That's an astonishing $793 a month.

And yes, you'd be contributing to a reduction in carbon emissions and air pollution. Nearly 30 percent of all global carbon dioxide emissions are due to transportation. By commuting via subway or bus, you'd be reducing your portion of the emissions by between 10 and 15 percent.

If you don't have reliable public transportation, consider the next best alternative: carpooling.

Carpooling is when a group shares rides together to work, taking turns driving on designated days. If you carpool with another individual, you may drive every other week. That means you've slashed your commuting expenses, especially gas consumption—in half. You may even be able to shorten your commute time, depending on where you live, by using the High Occupancy Vehicle lanes. These lanes are reserved for vehicles with more than one passenger.

You can cut your expenses even more by adding members to your arrangement. If you have four members, then you'd only have to drive the commute once a month.

If you carpool with three other individuals, you're reducing your commuting costs by 75 percent. If you're currently spending $160 a month on your commute, then you'd save $120 a month just with this simple act.

And, of course, with a carpool of four members, you're reducing, as a group, your carbon emissions by 75 percent. That's something to make you think about on your way to work (when it isn't your turn to drive).

I got it. You're not an overly friendly person. Or maybe more than a couple of people in a car make you claustrophobic. Understood. If carpooling and public transportation aren't for you, you can still cash in on monetary savings and aiding the environment.

Hop on That Bike

You could take your daily commute on a bicycle. Many

people do. According to experts, you can save 50 cents for every commute mile. This figure was calculated to include the gas used in getting to work, as well as depreciation and the vehicle's general maintenance.

Even if you don't commute, you may consider replacing a bike for a couple of errands a day. It's estimated that biking four miles a day instead of driving still puts a dent in your transportation costs. Believe it or not, this can save you up to $1,075 yearly or $89.60 monthly.

TURN THE CAR ENGINE OFF

When you allow your car to idle—leaving the engine on when the vehicle isn't moving—you're wasting fuel. There's a persistent belief that turning your car off and restarting it uses more fuel than letting it idle. That belief, however, is incorrect. If your car idles for longer than 10 seconds, it uses more gas than you had restarted.

There's also the myth that frequently restarting a car is adding unnecessary wear and tear on both the engine and its battery. That may have been true decades ago, but it causes very little harm to today's vehicles. In fact, some experts estimate the added wear costs no more than $10 a year.

This is much less costly than what it costs you in gas for an idling car. It adds up quickly, adding an extra $70 to $120 a year to fuel costs.

Allowing your car to idle will cost you approximately $10 a year in added wear but save you an average of $95 in gas. Your savings for the year amount to $85. That's an extra $7 a month that stays in your wallet.

WASH YOUR CAR BY HAND

You can save money on your car's maintenance in a straightforward step: skip the automated carwash.

That's right. Every time a vehicle goes through an in-bay carwash, it uses about 35 gallons of water. High-pressure touchless carwashes can use double that amount, and the tunnel version, which employs high-pressure applicators, uses upward of 120 gallons of water on your car.

You're paying a minimum of $10 for the basic wash and as much as $25 for options like an undercarriage wash, clear coat, wax, and the cleaning of the wheels.

The question is whether washing your car saves money and uses less water. Experts who've broken this argument down say yes. And that's even when you invest in a basic 16-ounce car-washing kit costing about $20. It's estimated that you can get 16 washes from this. That means supplies alone cost you approximately $1.25 per wash.

It will cost you less (even though you must put some time and elbow grease into the activity). But are you saving any water? According to one state environmental agency, washing your car uses about 116 gallons of water. While that's more than what a basic automatic wash uses, your cost will be less. The average U.S. household is estimated to pay one cent for a gallon of water. This means your water cost is $1.16 for a wash.

In total, you're spending $2.41 when you wash at home. That's a savings of $7.59 compared to a basic commercial wash. It's estimated that the average person washes their vehicle 13 times in a year. In a month, you can save about $8.22.

EVEN MORE WAYS TO SAVE

The following tips give you more ideas on how to save money and help the environment. It isn't easy to estimate the amount you can save. In most cases, the figures may vary too much to be useful to you. In other instances, there's not enough information to provide you with an accurate savings account. Rest assured, though, by following any (or all) of these ideas, you'll have more money in the bank at the end of the month.

1. Don't speed.

Aside from the chance of getting a speeding ticket and costing you big bucks, going to the speed limit can help save you gas. When your car runs too high, it uses more fuel. Every vehicle reaches optimal fuel usage at a different speed, but we can make some generalizations. Any time you go faster than 50 miles an hour, your gas mileage decreases. Rapidly. Every five miles an hour over 50, light-duty vehicle travel is the equivalent of paying 30 cents more than a gallon in gas. You can improve your car's fuel economy by 7 to 14 percent simply by driving 5 to 10 miles an hour slower.

2. Use cruise control.

If you're like me, you use this nifty feature to avoid speeding. But its ability to help you keep a constant speed also helps save on gas. Your vehicle uses the most energy when it accelerates. Cruise control avoids those hard accelerations and the hard stops, which also lowers your gas mileage.

3. Check your tires.

If your vehicle's tires aren't properly inflated, they reduce your gas mileage and cost you money. The National Highway Traffic Safety Administration (NHTSA) estimates you can save as much as 11 cents a gallon on fuel with proper tire pressure.

If you're not sure what's the optimum pressure is for your tires, there are two places you can look. Most car manufacturers place this information either on the driver-side door or on the door of the glove compartment.

Those minutes you check the tire pressure can add money to your bank account.

4. Declutter your car.

If you're like many of us, you probably have things in your car that may not belong there. If you carry extra weight in your vehicle, you're hurting your car's fuel efficiency.

It's no secret that fuel efficiency declines as vehicle weight increases. But that doesn't just refer to the weight of the car itself. Everything you have in the car increases weight.

Cleaning out your car is an easy way to get better gas mileage and save money.

The strategies presented in this chapter amount to an amazing $1,017.82 in savings in just one month. Obviously, you won't be able to use every one of these, as they present various methods of commuting to work. But even by using one or two of these tips, you'll be saving a considerable amount of money. And helping the planet at the same time.

In the next chapter, I will show you ways you can save money and help the environment when it comes to buying and maintaining your clothing. You'll be surprised how small actions add up quickly to big savings.

Chapter 6: Clothing: 5 Ways to Save as Much as $274.91 per Month

The average family spends approximately $2,000 a year on clothing. That's a large chunk of anyone's budget. Not only is apparel a drain on your budget, but it's also a drain on the planet as well.

The garment industry is one of the world's worst polluters. Just look at some statistics on how industry is depleting the planet's resources and injuring the environment.

- It takes 2,400 gallons of water to manufacture one pair of jeans

- Overall, the fashion industry consumes 93 billion cubic meters of water.

- The industry also produces approximately 10 percent of the global greenhouse gas emissions. That's more than all international flights and maritime shipping combined.

While these environmental facts seem overwhelming, and you may think the only solution is to wear fig leaves again, all is not lost. You may be surprised at the strategies you can incorporate into your daily life to save money and do your small part to help the planet.

ONLINE CONSIGNMENT

If you have children, you know how fast they can grow out of their clothes—sometimes before the end of a school year. It gets expensive to run out and buy new clothes for them. Then you're stuck with the old ones. Unless you have another younger child who'll be able to use them, what do you do with them?

I found the perfect solution a few years back: online consignment shops. Every year, I take the clothes the kids outgrew and clothes I discovered I no longer wear and put them up for sale on one of these sites.

On a few of these sites, I can get paid in cash, via PayPal or another cash app, or get store credit. I often opt for cash and then let that money sit in an account. I allow it to accumulate, and it becomes a clothes budget. My sale of unwanted and ill-fitting clothes morphs into the purchase of more. The beauty of this is that I'm taking less money out of my household budget.

Some families have earned upward of $500 monthly selling clothes on these apps. Let's say your family of four earns only $75 monthly. That's $75 you can put toward your clothes budget. It is considered savings. Congratulations.

Poshmark was one of the first online consignment shops, but now you have your choice. You may want to check out the following to see which would be best for you. I've listed the seven most popular and well-respected apps.

- Queenly

- The RealReal

- Vestiaire Collective

- Poshmark

- Kidizen

- ThredUp

- Fashionphile

SAVE WITH COST-PER-WEAR

Individuals keep a piece of clothing for about two years, according to several studies. What if you kept yours just a year longer? If you could do that, you'd not only reduce the carbon footprint of the garment by 20, maybe 30 percent, but you'd be saving money.

Believe it or not, there's a simple way of calculating how much you'd save. You just must figure out the cost-per-wear. It's a method to find the true price and value of your clothes based on the number of times you've worn them. You divide the cost of the clothing by the number of times you wore them.

Let's say you buy a women's blazer for work. That may cost you anywhere from $50 to $250, depending on where you shop. Let's work with an average price of $150. If you wore that once a week for two years, you would have worn it a total of 104 times. To find the cost-per-wear, you divide $150 by 104 times. Your cost-per-wear is about $1.44. Now, if you extend the life of that blazer by one year, you'd have worn it 156 times. That brings the cost-per-wear down to $0.96. That means every time you wore it, you'd save $0.48. In a year, you'd save nearly $75 in that extra year. That amounts to $6.24 a month.

If you did that with every item in your wardrobe, the savings would add up. And you don't need to clip any coupons.

SHOP THRIFT STORES

Thrift stores are chic these days, you know. More than 60 percent of all Gen X'ers shop in thrift stores for clothes. And if you want a painless way to save money on clothes and help the environment at the same time, you may want to give it a try yourself.

And if you're in the market for a handbag, you'll want

to look at a thrift store first. You can usually find beautiful designer bags for a fraction of the original cost. And no one will know where you bought it unless you tell them.

It's estimated that the average thrift store shopper saves an amazing $1,800 a year on clothes. That's $150 a month you still have in your pocket.

Rent that Dress

If you're like me, you hate spending money on a dress or other outfit you know you will only wear once. Have you thought about renting it instead? It's not a new idea. Men have had the option of renting suits and tuxedoes for their special occasions for a long time.

It's a relatively new concept for women's clothing, though. You can find online stores that rent the dress or suit of your dreams. You wear it and return it. It's that easy.

A formal dress for a wedding or a cocktail party can cost at least $250. But you can rent a similar (or nicer) dress from a site like Rent the Runway for an average of

$75. That's a savings of $175. If you're invited to two functions a year, you'd save $325 or a bit more than $27 a month.

And if you find you like the idea of renting, for a monthly fee, you can rent professional and casual clothes regularly. If you find an item you truly love, you have the option of purchasing it at a deeply discounted price.

SNATCH UP BRAND NAMES FOR LESS

You don't have to pay full price for name-brand clothing. Let that be your new mantra. When you shop at stores like Marshalls or Nordstrom Rack, you can discover high-quality, brand-name clothes for less—sometimes at 75 percent less.

Let's say that you only get a 50 percent discount on a piece of clothing. If the original price of the dress was $100 and you snatch it up for $50, you've saved $50. If you shop like that every quarter, four times a year, you can save $200 in a year. And the monthly savings come to about $16.67. That wouldn't be difficult to do if you're shopping for a family of four.

EVEN MORE WAYS TO SAVE

The list of ways to save on clothing is long and chockfull of savings, many of which are difficult to estimate accurately for the average family. But the following strategies are guaranteed to save you money while contributing to the health of the planet. How much is totally up to you.

1. Shop for quality.

Sure, you spend a bit more on quality items. That doesn't seem like a way to save money. But a well-made blazer or pair of jeans will last you longer and will lower your cost-per-wear ratio. I mentioned the average person wears an item of clothing for only two years. Upping that to three can save you money. And if you invest in quality garments, you may even be able to extend their life even longer. So yes, go for quality of price if it's an item you'll get a lot of use.

2. Swap clothes.

We've all heard of hand-me-downs, those clothes you get from your older siblings. Why not take a twist on that idea and do a clothes swap. Get together with friends with children the same age as yours and swap kids' items. You can also exchange adult clothing as well.

If you want to go big, why not organize one for your children's school. It would help everyone's budget, and it would certainly be a nice way to help the planet.

3. Repair your clothes first.

I'm not suggesting you become a seamstress. But, if a shirt or blouse is missing a button, well, most of us can figure out how to sew a new one. You can also fix a hole in the clothing too. If you have any questions about how to do it, there are plenty of YouTube videos. And sometimes you can sew something over the hole that not only covers it but gives it decorative flair.

4. Rethink how you wash clothes.

How you wash your clothes can help them last longer. Here are a few tips to get you started:

Use cold water when you can. Think of cold water as your new best-budget friend. It's less abrasive on fabrics than hot water. Not only that, but the chances of your clothing shrinking or stretching in cold water are much lower. And cold water will have your bright colors staying bright longer. Cold water also saves on your energy bill and, in turn, aids the environment.

Wash your clothes less. No, I'm not talking about wearing your jeans all month long. But you don't have to wash them after every wear. The rule of them is after you wear them three times, you should wash them. That is if you're not cleaning out a horse stall in them. By washing your clothes less, they don't wear out as fast. They don't go through all the tumbling in the washer with the abrasive detergent.

Wash your clothes inside out. By doing this, you can reduce their fading as well as preserve prints from cracking.

If you try all five tips in this chapter, you can save up to $274.91 monthly. Is that too much change all at once? Start small and slowly change your habits. Any step you take toward saving money is progress, regardless of how small. And it's also a step toward helping improve the environment. Baby-step your way to savings!

In the next chapter, I will show you ways in which you

can help the planet and save money on entertainment. It's a lot easier than you think.

Chapter 7: Entertainment: 7 Ways to Save as Much as $272.77 per Month

Just because you're on a budget doesn't mean you can't indulge in a little fun now and then. While it seems like the cost of everything connected to entertainment is rising—from books to movies and even board games, there are ways to enjoy yourself and save money, and in the process, help the environment.

The Library

When was the last time you visited your local library?

And if you have been there recently, did you notice all the materials it has? Today's library isn't your grandmother's quiet tomb filled with card catalogs and librarians shushing you.

No, today, you can rent just about anything at your local library, not just books. Looking for a good movie? You can find one here. Tired of playing all the games you own? Do not worry; the library has you covered.

The beautiful part is that you can borrow all of these for free. Where else can you wander around and take out merchandise on a promise to return for nothing?

How do you save with the library?

Hopefully, you're a step ahead of me and are already counting how you can save by using this wonderful resource. Let's start with books, the traditional stock in the library trade. You can borrow the latest bestsellers, which will not cost you a dime. It sure beats the prices at the big chain bookstores.

If you read only three books a year (and so many of us read more than that), you spend about $46.50 a year, based on the average paperback is about $15.50. You don't pay a cent if you forget about buying and borrowing those books from the library. That averages $3.87 a month. But that's only a single individual reading.

If you have a family of four, you'd quadruple your savings to $15.48 a month. But you'll probably start reading more this way, so your savings will be even greater.

You can also save money on board games. Borrowing them from the library is a great way to save money. It's also a great way to try out a game. You can buy if you love it enough and think you'll get your money's worth.

The average price of a board game is about $30. You can find some for as low as $20 and as high as $45 or greater. And the average family buys five new games a year, according to game board industry statistics.

What if you borrowed them from the library instead of buying five new games? You'd save $100 a year, or $8.34 a month—or more. You may decide to try out any number of games.

When was the last time you saw a movie at a theater? The average price of a movie ticket is now $11, not counting the popcorn, about $8 and the soda, about $6. A night at the movies will cost one person about $24. If you're a couple, that's $48.

Yes, there are nights you want to treat yourself. But you can also visit the library and borrow a movie. When you make your popcorn and buy soda, you have a similar experience. You don't have anyone talking through the movie. Microwave popcorn costs as little as 50 cents a bag, and the average two-liter soda costs about $2.50.

Your in-home movie night costs $3.00 for the two of you. You save $21. If you go to the movies thrice a year, you save $63 or $5.25 a month. If you have children, you'll save even more.

Love to read and want to keep books?

If you're like me, you may want to keep the books you read rather than return them to a library. I also have a problem reading books in the three-week window the library gives me.

That's why I buy many of my books used. If your city has an independently used bookstore, that's an excellent place to start your search. You're not only helping the environment by buying used. You'll be supporting a small business. And you'll be saving money.

If you can't find a physically used bookstore, you can find them online. One of my favorites is https://www.thriftbooks.com/. Here, you'll find a wide variety of used books. The average cost of a used book is about $4.55. Of course, some authors are in more demand and are a bit more expensive, but you can still find books for less than at new bookstores. And you can get free shipping.

If you buy five used books a year, that's an average cost of $22.75. Compare that to five new books at any bookstore, where you'd pay an average of $73. That's savings of $50.25 or $4.18 a month.

Free Movies

You read that right. You can see a movie (or two or three) for free and enjoy the great outdoors. Many communities have a "Movies under the Stars" program where they show great cinema outside at no cost. Most of these are family-friendly.

This is a beautiful family fun activity for the summer. Check out your local community bulletin boards or search online for a program near you. You can create anticipation by planning what movies you'd like to see. Put these on the calendars.

If you do go to the movies, you'll want to be sure to pack your snacks. Bring some drinks in a cooler and chips or other munchies to snack on during the show. This is much cheaper than buying popcorn and soda at a movie theater.

Remember to ensure every family member has something to sit on. Adults may want chairs, but children may be happy with a blanket, depending on where the show is held. Some shows are held in parking lots. I'm not sure even children would want to sit on a blanket on hard cement. Find out ahead of time where the movie is playing and plan your seating accordingly.

How much do you save?

Your only expense is the snacks. A couple of chips, a pack of mini-candy bars and a six-pack of soda cost under $20 if you buy them at a dollar store. Compare this to the price of four tickets and food from a theater's concession stand, about $24 a person; for a family of four, that's $96. You can save $76 on one movie. If you go monthly during the summer and see three, you'll save $228 in a year alone on this program. If you spread that savings over a year, that's $19 a month.

FREE CLASSES OR WORKSHOPS

Do you love yoga but can't afford the $15 a session? Then I have a deal for you. Contact your community center or multi-generational center to find their schedule. Most centers offer yoga, and it's usually free. If your community center offers it twice a week, you can save $30. And you'll improve your health. If you do it 50 weeks out of a year (everyone must take a vacation), you'll save $1,500 or about $125 monthly.

If you're not into yoga, you can find many free classes and other activities at your local community or multi-generational center—painting, cooking, crafts and more.

CABLE COSTS

The average cost of cable television has skyrocketed to $200 a month. That's much money to pay, especially when so many channels never get watched. I have a list of about five channels I've watched regularly on cable TV.

You should cut the cord on the cable. Don't panic. I know it's been a staple of American homes for nearly 40 years. But it's outgrown its usefulness.

What do you do instead?

Start with just essential internet for about $75 a month. From there, add two or three streaming services. Choose the ones you know you'll use the most. For example, Netflix has movies to please everyone, from Dad and Mom to the kids. Netflix's cheapest subscription is a little under $7. The standard subscription is $15.49.

If you have children, you'll probably want to stream Disney+. It's only $13.99 a month.

If you still think you're missing something, consider the many free streaming services available, starting with Pluto. It's the internet's answer to cable TV, offering more than 250 free channels.

You can also choose any or all the free options of the following services:

- YouTube

- Hula

- Peacock

- Tubi

- Hoopla (courtesy of your local library)

- Popcornfix

- Vudu

- Crackle

I've only listed a few of these. An internet search will undoubtedly reveal more that suits your family's viewing tastes.

How much money do you save?

If you take the standard Netflix and the Disney+ channels, along with your $75 internet fee, you'd be paying $104.48 a month compared to the $200 cable fee. That's a yearly savings of $1,146.24 a year or $95.52 a month.

Even More Ways to Save

There are even more ways you can save on your entertainment budget. The following strategies are sure to help, even though it's difficult to estimate the amount you could save.

1. Organize a game night.

You can organize or even host a game night among your friends. There's no need to feel obligated to have a meal. Just ask people over in the evening with their favorite game. If everyone brings some snacks, there should be plenty of food.

This can replace a movie night or a dinner out. And you're keeping the bonds of friendship strong.

2. Host a potluck party.

When you host (or even organize) a potluck dinner, you won't be stuck with the expense of providing the entire meal. You can assign individuals to bring a specific type of dish, like the entrée, sides, and desserts. Or you can offer the entrée and have everyone else get something—

and see what happens.

It's cheaper than making an entire meal and more affordable than hosting friends to a dinner you've made.

3. Discover the Great Outdoors.

When we think about doing things, we often think about indoor activities. Instead of going to the movies on a Saturday afternoon with the kids, why not take them hiking or biking? You can pack a picnic lunch or just snacks. Why not spend the day outside?

If you live near a national park, you may want to check out its "Free Entrance Days." About six times a year, the national park services offer free entry. It's a great way to explore the Great Outdoors.

4. Volunteer.

Wait… hear me out on this one. I want to see a concert but don't want to pay the admission fee. Why not become a volunteer?

If you love theater, why not volunteer at your local community theater? You'll get to see the play without putting out any money. You may find you like being an usher or taking tickets. And one thing's for sure: local theater can always use the help.

Using all 7 tips for entertaining, you can save as much as $272.77 a month. That's not counting the 4 other tips that are difficult to calculate. Even if you only use two or three of these, you're still reducing your entertainment costs.

Follow me to the next chapter, where I will discuss how you can save on your home renovations and décor while aiding the environment.

Chapter 8: Renovations and Interior Decorating: 6 Ways to Save as Much as $235.65 per Month

So much of an average home is made of wood, from the furniture to the floors and everything in between. Sadly, one-sixth of all global carbon emissions are due to the mismanagement of the clearing of forests.

Forests are power weapons in the fight against climate change. They possess the unique ability to absorb up to one-tenth of all global emissions. While the furniture isn't the most significant culprit, its impact shouldn't be underestimated. Wood is a limited resource.

The good news is that it doesn't take a lot of effort on your part to help become part of the solution. You're already searching for ways to save money on renovations and decorating. Implementing a few strategies can help slow deforestation and keep a few more dollars in your pocket.

I've presented ways you can save money on renovating and decorating them that will help save the trees and conserve energy, too. Let's get started.

INSULATION

If you're remodeling your current home or considering building a new one, insulate it. You'll not only save money every year, but by using less energy, you're helping the environment.

In the winter, insulation slows the heat escape from the

house and keeps the hot air out in the summer. Experts say this is the best way to have consistently lower energy bills by an average of 20 percent year-round.

Sadly, 90 percent of single-family homes don't have enough insulation. The odds are good that yours is among them—especially if it was built before 1960.

You can choose from various types, depending on what kind of building you live in. I will talk about a few of them below:

1. Cavity wall.

Heat escaping through the wall accounts for approximately one-third of a house's heat loss. If your home was built before 1990, it likely lacks cavity-wall insulation.

2. Floor

This type of insulation is perfect if you live on the ground floor or above a space that's not heated, like a garage. You can even use this installation if your floor is concrete.

3. Roof and loft.

Almost as much heat is lost through the roof as through the walls. A full 25 percent of it is escaping through the roof or loft.

4. Solid wall.

If your home is older, it may have solid external walls. You can insulate these, but it costs more than cavity-wall insulation. Nevertheless, it's worth the investment.

5. Pipes, radiators, hot-water tanks.

Here's an insulation you can do yourself. Protecting exposed pipes, radiators, and your hot-water tank can save more than you think. This type of insulation is inexpensive and can be found at your local home improvement or hardware store.

6. Draft-proofing

Another method of insulation is draft proofing. It's nothing more than blocking gaps that allow cold air to sneak in the winter and the hot air in the summer. You can do this by putting towels at the bottom of the outside doors, where there's that little gap.

And don't forget the fireplace. About four percent of your heat loss occurs in the chimney. But you can reduce that by installing a chimney balloon. As its name implies, it inflates to hug the chimney's walls. Because it's such a snug fit, it holds itself in place. It also has a small vent to allow the structure to breathe. If you want to use the fireplace, simply deflate and remove it. When you're done, you can put it back in.

Home insulation projects can be as inexpensive as $500 or cost as much as $2,160, depending on the size of your home and the type of insulation you choose. But, when you're in this price range, you'll install the attic or crawl space insulation yourself.

Let's take the average of these two numbers, $1,330, and use that as the cost of insuring your home. Your yearly savings will be $280 a year, or $23.40 a month. You won't recoup your investment in the first year. It'll take you nearly five years to see the savings. But you will see it. And from the moment you install the insulation, you'll reduce your carbon footprint.

Buy Used Furniture

If you're looking for furniture, why not think used?

There are plenty of vintage and second-hand furniture stores that have near-pristine pieces. Purchasing these can save you money.

Looking for a dining-room table and chairs. A medium-priced set at a new furniture store can cost you about $1,500. But you can buy something similar from a private seller or a second-hand store for as little as $500. That's a savings of $1,000. If you extend that savings to your yearly budget, you're saving $83.33 a month.

And that's only one item. You can also find end tables and dressers as well. If you want, you can furnish every room in your home with used furniture. And only you will be the wiser.

Make Your Furniture

This is a bold suggestion. But you can save money by making your furniture. The plus? It will be precise to your taste.

You can also make it an environmentally friendly project by using reclaimed wood. The used wood also lends an authentic, earthy style.

Some home improvement stores offer free classes if you want to try it.

According to those who've built one, you can make a kitchen table for about $80. The equivalent table is brand new and costs about $900. That's a savings of $820. If you spread that throughout your yearly budget, you'd have a monthly savings of $68.34.

REPAINT YOUR FURNITURE

You really love that piece of furniture, but it's seen better days. Or perhaps you've just added new (or your homemade items), and it doesn't match anymore. Instead of spending $350 on a moderate-priced new dresser, why not paint the old one?

You can buy an entire gallon of paint for about $50. If the original paint is flaked or peeling, you'll want to sand it. The sandpaper will cost you about $15. Don't you have a paintbrush? You can buy one online or at a home improvement store that is perfect for your project for about $10. Your dresser can have a brand-new look for a maximum investment of $75. That's a $275 savings from buying a new one. Take that money you saved and spread it throughout your yearly budget, and you have a monthly savings of $22.91.

REPURPOSE ORDINARY CONTAINERS

If you're redecorating or just looking for a new touch for your home, consider adding a few live plants. And then, consider potting them in containers you already have. Think teapots, ice buckets, large cans, and even colanders make great planters.

You can even use a container typically found in that room. A teapot or colander would be a great kitchen or dining room addition. You should use an ice bucket in your den. If you paint a large can, you can place it in any room.

If you buy a new planter, you'd spend an average of $20 (perhaps more). If you use a container you already have, the cost is nothing. And $20 spread over your yearly decorating budget amounts to a monthly savings of $1.67.

Bamboo Flooring

The next time you need to install a floor, consider bamboo. You read that right. It's a less expensive alternative to hardwood floors and environmentally friendly.

Bamboo technically isn't a tree but a woody grass. Because of this, it grows much quicker than trees. It's one of the fastest-growing plants in the world. One species even holds The Guinness Book of Records for growing 35 inches daily.

But wait...there's more good news about bamboo. It is typically grown naturally, without the aid of chemical fertilizers. It's practically pest- and disease-free. It absorbs greenhouse gases and pumps out much oxygen. Bamboo also needs only modest amounts of water to grow.

Hardwood flooring costs an average of $6 square feet for materials like hard maple or red oak. Bamboo flooring only costs an average of $4 a square foot. There's no significant difference in installations between bamboo and hardwood.

The average living room size is 216 square feet. Installing hardwood floors into this room would cost $1,296 for materials alone, compared to bamboo flooring, which would cost $864. Installing the bamboo floor would save you $432. If you spread that throughout the year, your monthly savings in your renovation budget would be $36.

Ways to Save More

I've included the following strategies to help you save money on your home renovations and décor, even though I can't give you a reasonable estimate of how much these ideas may save you. But if you see one or two that seem good to you, you can research to discover how they'll help your budget and the environment.

1. Don't toss those wallpaper scraps.

Wallpaper scraps make the perfect accent for your rooms. Instead of buying new lamps to match your new room, you can cover your existing lampshades with what you have left of your wallpaper. These leftovers also bring new life to a dull light switch cover. You can also use these linings for your drawers. The possibilities are nearly limitless. Think of the money you can save.

2. Swap, don't toss.

The next time you're thinking of getting new (or used) furniture or room décor, don't toss it in the trash. Instead, why not go that extra mile and check to see if someone else can use it?

You can do this in several ways. First, you can get together with your friends to see if they have any items they no longer want. And you can swap them out. Or you can go online and offer them for free on any number of community websites. Some of the most well-known are Facebook Marketplace and Offer Up.

You'll be giving the environment a little boost. Your items won't end up in the landfill. You'll also be helping someone who can genuinely use the item.

3. Water-saving faucets.

Water-saving faucets and showerheads can help you reduce your water use. If you're renovating, you want to consider these. These faucets mix air with water flow, giving the feel that you have a full flow even though your volume is reduced. You'll save money on your water bill and help the environment.

4. Install a sun tunnel.

When you renovate, consider installing a sun tunnel. Its penetration in the roof allows more light into your home naturally. And don't worry, it doesn't have to be a sunny day for you to enjoy it. The acrylic dome of the device captures the light, magnifies it, and then sends it down the tube into something called the light diffuser. The interior of the tube is polished and acts like a continuous mirror, channeling the sun's light down without losing any intensity. While the light isn't as strong as direct sunlight, it's still strong enough to brighten any room. You'll need less lighting in your room, reducing your energy bill and helping the planet.

If you implement the six strategies presented in this chapter, you can save as much as $199.65 monthly.

Follow me to the next chapter, where I show you how to save even more with miscellaneous tips.

Chapter 9: Miscellaneous Tips: 4 Ways to Save as Much as $97.33 per Month

I've discussed so many ways to save money and aid the environment. You'd think there'd be nothing left to share. Surprise. There are still several more ways in a variety of areas.

I wanted to ensure you had these in your arsenal of money-saving, planet-aiding strategies. Let's get started.

GROW YOUR VEGETABLES

What if I told you it doesn't take a large garden of your own to experience significant monthly savings on your grocery bill?

Each visit to the grocery store costs more than the time before. Nowhere is that more evident than in the produce section. Then, to add insult to injury, you forget about the broccoli or the lettuce in the back of the refrigerator and must throw it out. What a waste.

You can see how growing your garden and your family's favorite vegetables can save you money.

How much money? Even a tiny 4-foot by 4-foot square garden can save you as much as $160 a year. Plus, you'll probably have enough to give to your friends. One home gardener said she harvests up to 40 pounds of onions, carrots, and sweet potatoes yearly.

By growing your food, you won't have to worry about toxic pesticides. Your food will be organic (and you know how expensive organically grown vegetables are).

You don't need to build raised beds if you have well-drained soil. All you need to do is lay out the garden beds and create paths around them to harvest quickly.

If you don't have soil suitable for growing, you will have some expenses initially. You'll want to frame the bed with 2" x 8" treated wood. For the 4' x 4' size I mentioned earlier, the wood would cost about $20. Filling it with gardening potting soil costs about $65.

That's a total of $85 for an initial investment. Still, you'll save $75 on groceries your first year or $6.25 a month. You can save even more if you make your garden a bit bigger.

You'll also be helping the environment. Your garden does its part in reducing carbon emissions from burning fossil fuels. No plastic packaging is involved since the veggies go from your garden straight to your table.

CLOTH DIAPERS

If you're a parent of a three-year-old or younger child, I don't have to tell you how many diapers the little person can go through. Every parent spends a ton of money on disposable diapers for about the first three years of their child's life.

Here's a quick breakdown of the numbers as the child ages:

Up to 6 months, a child goes through about 10 diapers a day or a total of 1,825. Once they reach 6 months, that number drops to about 8 a day until 18 months old. That's about 2,920 during that growing stage. Once they're 18 months, they only use about 6 diapers a day until they reach three years. That amounts to 3,285 diapers during this growth period.

A child will go through 8,030 diapers before he steps into real underpants. And the cost associated with that is quite astounding. On average, one disposable diaper costs about 25 cents. This means that in those three years, you'll spend an average of $2,007.50 on diapers.

This would make any parent think about cloth diapers. While one diaper costs an average of $18, you'd only need to buy about two dozen—24—to start with. That cost is only $432. You may be able to use these for the entire three years.

Your savings would be $1575.50 for the three years. This amounts to $525.17 a year or $43.76 a month.

But wait...there's more. If you have a second child, you may be able to use some of these cloth diapers for them, too. The savings continue.

And we haven't talked about disposable diapers' impact on the environment. It may take up to 500 years for diapers to degrade; all the while, they create toxic gases like methane.

INVEST IN AN ENERGY-EFFICIENT WATER HEATER

If your water heater is old, it may cost you more than you think. An energy-efficient water heater, like an energy-star certified one, can cut your electric bill by $470 a year.

The average water heat costs about $1,324. You'll pay more for an energy-efficient one since they cost an average of $2,250. Your upfront cost will be about $926 more. But the water heater will pay for itself in two years. And after that, you'll enjoy a monthly savings of $39.17 on your energy bill.

RECYCLE YOUR CELL PHONE

It's confession time. How many old cell phones do you have lying around the house? At least one, if you're like me. And really, what can you do with an old phone?

You can get paid for recycling. Several websites will buy the phone you use from you. Not only benefits your wallet, but it also helps the environment immensely. It's estimated that 151 million cell phones end up in landfills or are incinerated yearly. In the United States, up to 40 percent of the heavy metals in landfills come from cell phones.

This doesn't just hurt the environment. It hurts humans as well. E-waste, as it's called, releases a host of contaminants, including arsenic, lead, mercury, and zinc.

How much is your used phone worth?

Depending on the site you use and the make and model of your phone, you're likely to receive as little as $25 to as much as $340. The average individual receives about

$97.83. If you spread this over your yearly budget, you save $8.15 a month.

Ways to Save More

You can save even more by using the following strategies. I can't estimate the amount you'd save because that could vary depending on your habits. But you can rest assured that every little effort you make will help with your budget and the environment.

1. Printer ink.

It's frustrating to run out of ink. And it seems that happens far too often. An ounce of ink costs more than the equivalent amount in gas for your car or even for Dom Perignon Champagne. When you view it from this perspective, anything you can do to stretch that cartridge farther is worth it.

And there are two strategies you can use starting now. First, use the draft mode on the printer for items that aren't that important. This model is still legible and perfect for items like recipes.

The second change you can make is to change the font you type in. You may find this hard to believe, but if you switch from the Arial font (which happens to be my favorite) to Times New Roman, that cartridge will last 27 percent longer.

2. Skip the printing process.

An even better strategy is to avoid printing anything out. Whenever possible, avoid printing anything. What about that recipe? You could call the document on your tablet and follow it there.

Not only will you be saving on ink, you'll be saving on paper, doing your part to help slow down the planet's deforestation.

3. Use outdoor solar lighting.

If you're currently lighting your home's sidewalk with regular lights, you may want to consider installing solar lighting. The lights will charge all day and then be lit during the night. If you have a motion-sensor security light, you can install a solar-powered one. That will save on your electric bill and help conserve energy. And you don't forfeit your security.

4. Secrets of the refrigerator.

The refrigerator keeps secrets that need to come out in the open. Two of these will help your budget and the planet.

Most refrigerators are energy efficient when temperatures are between 35- and 38 degrees Fahrenheit. Most freezers reach peak efficiency when temperatures are between 0- and 5 degrees Fahrenheit.

Your refrigerator doesn't like it when packed to brimming with food. It works best when about three-quarters full of space around the items for the cold air to circulate. And yes, where do you store your items matters. Dairy, ready-to-eat products, and leftovers stay fresh longer when stored on the top shelf. Meat and fish stay fresher longer when stored on the lowest shelf. Fruits and vegetables are best stored in the bottom drawers.

If you implement all four strategies in this chapter, you can save as much as $97.32 monthly. That's not counting the tips that I couldn't calculate savings for. But you know your habits and lifestyle and which will work for you.

CONCLUSION

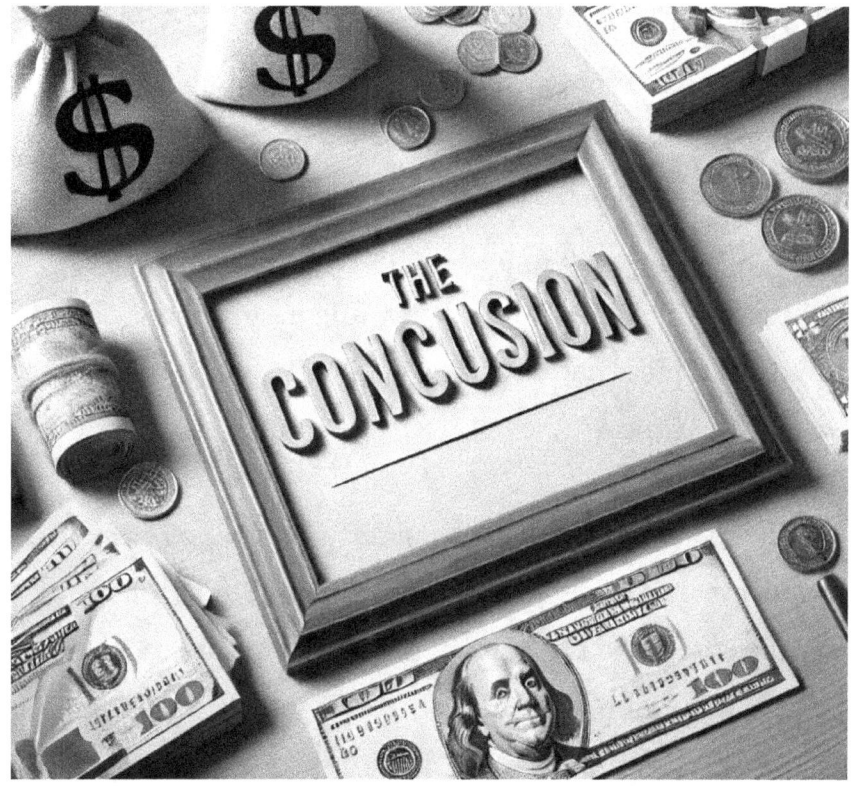

Congratulations on your willingness to save money and help the planet in the process. Know that every action, however small, goes toward a healthier world. And the icing on the cake is that your budget stretches much farther.

I want to leave you with one more trick in your quest to save money. It's a simple one. And it's totally up to you how much money you can save using it. It doesn't require any special appliances or even buy any new products.

Mindful shopping is the act of keeping your attention on the present moment while you're contemplating your purchases. When you shop this way, you'll bring your full awareness to your tasks. By doing this, you can avoid unhealthy spending habits. You know, the ones—the impulse purchases, the overspending associated with them, and, most notably, for the planet, supporting unethical brands.

When you shop, stop to consider whether you need the product or if it's something you want. It'll take some practice to ignore the sales signs. But with practice, you'll be able to. (Be kind to yourself while you're practicing.)

Choose quality or quantity. The item costs more initially, but it will last longer. In the final analysis, you'll save money.

Research the environmental effect of an item before you purchase it. If it's not contributing to the good of the planet, find an alternative.

Keep your gift-buying simple. A smaller, less expensive

gift offered after giving thought to the recipient is more appreciated than a costly gift that probably won't even be used.

Add the habit of mindfully shopping to the money-saving strategies in this book, and you'll find more money for the things near and dear to your heart. And Mother Nature will thank you.

I'm honored that you've trusted me to help you develop your new activities, habits, and attitude toward what's important. The last change will naturally occur.

Good luck in all your endeavors!

www.ingramcontent.com/pod-product-compliance
Lightning Source LLC
Chambersburg PA
CBHW071031240526
45469CB00006BD/2175